The Magic School Bus
At the Waterworks

The Magic School Bus
At the Waterworks

By Joanna Cole   Illustrated by Bruce Degen

SCHOLASTIC INC.
New York   Toronto   London   Auckland   Sydney

*The author and illustrator wish to thank Nancy Zeilig and
the technical services staff at American Water Works Association,
Denver, Colorado, for their help in preparing this book.*

ISBN 0-590-40360-5

24 23   2 3 4 5 6 7/9

Printed in the U.S.A.   08

To Rachel

J.C.

For Uncle Jerry,
the Water Chemist

B.D.

Our class really has bad luck.
This year, we got Ms. Frizzle,
the strangest teacher in school.

We don't mind Ms. Frizzle's strange dresses.
Or her strange shoes.
It's the way she acts that really gets us.
Ms. Frizzle makes us grow green mold
on old pieces of bread.
She makes us build clay models of garbage dumps,
draw diagrams of plants and animals,
and read five science books a week.

9

Other classes go on trips to the zoo,
or even the circus.
Guess where we went on our class trip.
To the waterworks!

10

And to get ready for the trip,
Ms. Frizzle made us
spend a whole month in the library.
We had to find out exactly
how our city gets its water —
down to the last drop.
We also had to collect
ten interesting facts about water.

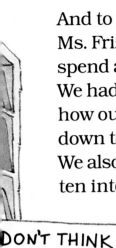

Water Fact #2
by Tim

Water is the only substance that is found in the form of a liquid, a solid, and a gas in nature.

LIQUID (WATER)

SOLID (ICE)

GAS (WATER VAPOR)

OH NO! NOT THE OCTOPUS DRESS!

LET'S PRE
WE DON'
KNOW HE

In the parking lot,
the old school bus was waiting.
To our surprise,
there was no bus driver.
Instead, The Friz herself
was behind the wheel.

12

At the end of the block
the bus went into a dark tunnel.
When we came out, something amazing
had happened.
The bus looked a lot different.
We looked different, too.
Everyone was wearing
a scuba diving outfit!
Even Ms. Frizzle.

ANT
MOMMY.

13

Ms. Frizzle was the only one
who didn't seem to notice the change.
She just drove on.
In the middle of a bridge,
the bus started ...

to rise into ...

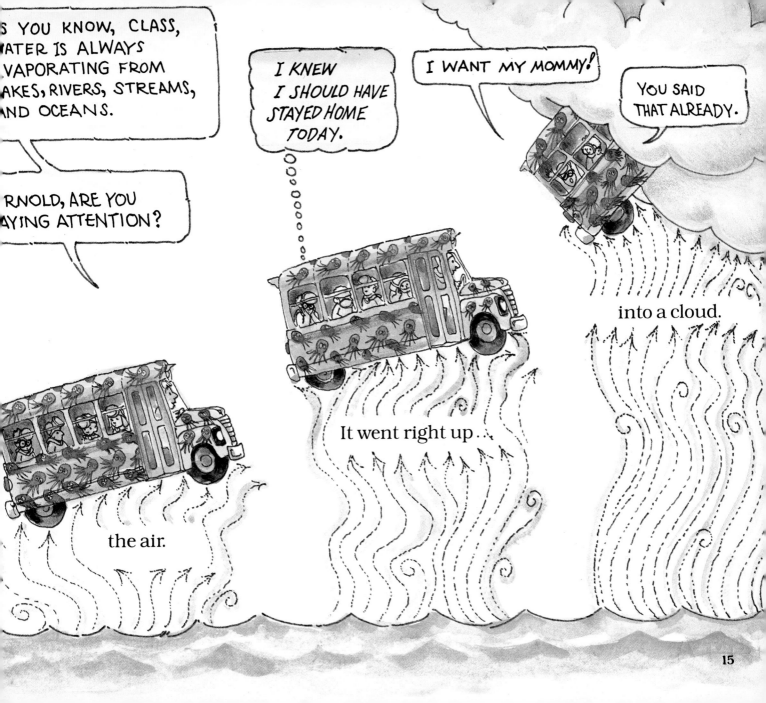

15

Then Ms. Frizzle did
the weirdest thing ever.
She told everybody to get
out of the bus!
The kids didn't want to go.
But Frizzie threatened to give
extra homework if we didn't.

I'LL TAKE THE
HOMEWORK.

Some kids stuck their heads
out of the cloud and looked down.
There were mountains down there!
And the cloud was going higher
every minute.

Before long, each kid was
the size of a raindrop.
In fact, each kid was
in a raindrop.
The drops began to fall.
Ms. Frizzle's class was raining!

In no time, we reached
the reservoir
that holds water
for our city.
We were going into
the water purification system.
This class trip was
not so boring after all!

EVERGREEN TREES KEEP I
AND LEAVES FROM BLOWIN
INTO THE RESERVOIR.

FENCE KEEPS PEOPLE
AND ANIMALS FROM
DIRTYING THE RESERVOIR.

THIS IS GREAT!

WHAT'S

ALUM

YUCK!

WATCH OUT FOR THE GLOBS!

The water in the reservoir
was pretty dirty.
We were covered with dirt and mud.
"Follow me to the mixing basin,"
shouted Ms. Frizzle.
In the mixing basin, a clumping substance
called alum was added to the water.
The alum formed globs,
and all the dirt and mud stuck
to the globs.

MIXING BASIN

SETTLING BASIN

22

WATER FACT #6
by Ralph
Less than 1 percent of all the water on earth is fresh water that we can drink. The rest is salty water in the oceans or frozen water in glaciers or ice caps.

"On to the settling basin!" ordered The Friz.
There the globs sank to the bottom, and the clean water flowed off the top.
Now we were on our way to the filter.

This was the sand-and-gravel filter
that takes out any impurities
still in the water.
We were impurities,
we couldn't get through!
Luckily, Ms. Frizzle showed us
a special way around the filter.
When the water came out of the filter,
it was sparkling clear.

WE CAN'T
GET THROUGH!

WE'LL BE STUCK
IN THE WATERWORKS
FOREVER!

OUCH

24

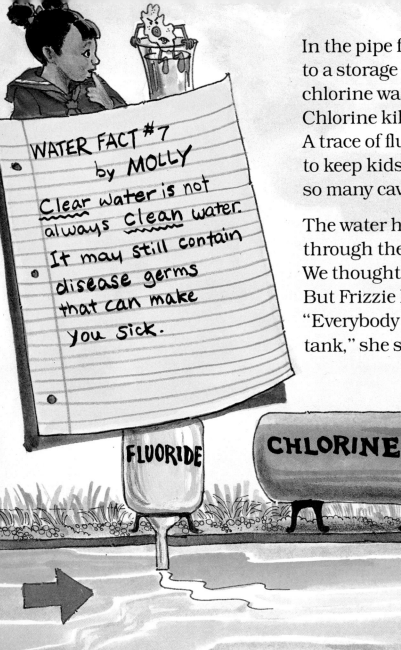

WATER FACT #7
by MOLLY
Clear water is not always clean water.
It may still contain disease germs that can make you sick.

In the pipe from the filter to a storage tank, a chemical called chlorine was added to the water. Chlorine kills any remaining disease germs. A trace of fluoride was also added to keep kids from getting so many cavities.

The water had come all the way through the purification system. We thought our class trip was over. But Frizzie had other ideas. "Everybody into the storage tank," she shouted.

FLUORIDE

CHLORINE

Then we went into water mains,
the pipes that run under
the city streets.

THE FORCE OF WATER
AS IT MOVES THROUGH
THE PIPES IS CALLED

WATER PRESSURE.

GO WITH THE FLOW, KIDS.

28

EEEEK!

When a seventh-grader
turned on a faucet
in the girls' bathroom,
we came splashing out.
The building was our school!
We were back!
We were our regular size again!
We were dressed in normal clothes again!
(Except for Ms. Frizzle, of course.)

Back in the classroom,
Ms. Frizzle acted as if
nothing strange had happened.
She started feeding the class lizard.
And she put us to work right away.
We had to make a chart
showing how water gets
to the homes and buildings
in our city.

DOWN, GIRL.

When Arnold drew a picture of
a kid inside a raindrop,
Ms. Frizzle said,
"Where do you *get* these
crazy ideas, Arnold?"

WATER EVAPORATES
FROM LAKES AND
RIVERS...

1

1
WATER
EVAPORATES
FROM LAKES,
RIVERS, AND
OCEANS.

2
CLOUDS OF
WATER VAPOR
FORM IN
SKY.

3
RAIN FALLS
TO EARTH.
SOME FALLS
INTO STREAMS.

4
SOME STREAMS
RUN INTO
CITY'S
RESERVOIR.

5
IN MIXING
BASIN
DIRT AND MUD
STICK TO
ALUM CLUMPS.

6
IN SETT
BASI
CLUMPS O
AND DIR
SINK TO
BOTTO

ALUM

RESERVOIR   MIXING BASI

7
...-AND-
...VEL FILTER
...S OUT
...ST
...PURITIES.

8
IN PIPE TO
STORAGE TANK
FLUORIDE IS ADDED
FOR STRONG TEETH.
CHLORINE IS
ADDED TO KILL
EVERY LAST
DISEASE GERM.

9
PURE WATER
IS HELD IN
A STORAGE
TANK.

10
WATER MAINS
CARRY WATER
UNDER CITY
STREETS...

11
...TO OUR
HOMES
AND
BUILDINGS.

STORAGE TANK

...D AND GRAVEL
...ILTER

FLUORIDE   CHLORINE

WATER MAINS

Here is how our water chart turned out.

Later that day,
we saw the old bus
in the school parking lot.
How did *that* get there?
Did we only imagine going through
the water supply system?
Would we ever find out
what *really* happened?

THE LAST TIME
I SAW THAT BUS,
IT WAS IN A CLOUD
...I THINK...

36

Ms. Frizzle says we'll be studying
volcanos next.
This makes us all
feel a little nervous!
After all, with a teacher
like Ms. Frizzle,
anything can happen.

VOLCANO

THERE AREN'T ANY
VOLCANOS AROUND
HERE, ARE THERE?

NOTES FROM THE AUTHOR
(FOR *SERIOUS* STUDENTS ONLY)

The following notes are for serious students who do not like any kidding around when it comes to science facts. If you read these pages, you will be able to tell which facts in this book are true, and which were put in by the author as jokes. (This will also help you decide when to laugh while reading this book.)

On page 8: The green mold that grows on old bread is actually made up of tiny one-celled plants. It *cannot* talk or make any sound whatever.

On page 9: Plants do *not* have hands, *nor* do they wear sunglasses, and the soil does *not* contain burgers, fries, or shakes.

On page 13: Going through a dark tunnel will *not* cause you to wear a scuba diving outfit.

On pages 14-15: The force of gravity keeps a school bus firmly on the ground. It *cannot* rise into the air and enter a cloud, no matter how much you want to miss school that day.

On pages 16-31: Children *cannot* shrink and enter raindrops, fall into streams, or pass through the water purification system. And boys and girls *cannot* come out of the faucet in the girls' bathroom. (Anyone knows boys are not allowed in there.)

On pages 34-35: Your town or city may not get its water from a mountain reservoir, and the purification process may be slightly different from the one in this book. Many towns get water from rivers, lakes, or wells. Do you know where your water comes from and how it is purified?

On page 36: Once a bus is left behind in a cloud, it *cannot* suddenly appear in the school parking lot all by itself. Obviously, someone has to go back to the cloud and drive it home.